To the Quick

Also by Heather McHugh

Dangers
A World of Difference
D'Après Tout: Poems by Jean Follain

Wesleyan Poetry

Heather McHugh

To the Quick

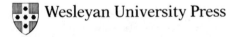 Wesleyan University Press

Poems in this book originally appeared in these magazines: *American Poetry Review, Antaeus, The Atlantic, Harvard Magazine, Kayak, The New Republic, The Paris Review, Science 84, Seneca Review, Tendril;* and these books: *The Generation of 2000: Contemporary American Poets, The Morrow Anthology of Younger American Poets,* and *New American Poets of the 80's.* The poem "In a World of Taking, the Mistake" appeared originally in *The New Yorker.* "Animal Song" appeared in the *Antaeus Anthology.* The Rilke poems were inspired by his Poèmes Français, *Sämtliche Werke* (Zweiter Band, Gedichte: Zweiter Teil, Insel-Verlag, 1958).

Emily Dickinson's "To flee from memory" reprinted by permission of the publishers, from *The Poems of Emily Dickinson,* edited by Thomas H. Johnson, Harvard University Press, copyright © 1951, 1955, 1979, 1983, by the President and Fellows of Harvard College.

Library of Congress Cataloging-in-Publication Data
McHugh, Heather, 1948—
  To the quick.
  (Wesleyan poetry)
  i. Title. ii. Series.
PS3563.A311614C87 1987   811'.54   85-29504
ISBN 0-8195-5156-2 (alk. paper)
ISBN 0-8195-6162-2 (pbk. : alk. paper)

All inquiries and permissions requests should be addressed to University Press of New England, Hanover, New Hampshire 03755.

Manufactured in the United States of America

5 4 3 2

Cover art: "Untitled" (1982-1984) by Robert Longo

"For Greg and Bryan,
abidingly"

To flee from memory
Had we the Wings
Many would fly
Inured to slower things unaccustomed
Birds with surprise
Would scan the cowering Van
Of men escaping
From the mind of man

EMILY DICKINSON

She describes
things that are
dangerous - a flock
of memories
attempting to escape.

Thanks to the Waco Diner in Eastport, Maine, and to the Last Exit on Brooklyn, in Seattle, Washington, I was able to take my time over months of notebooks, and a few coffees; patience, in proprietors, amounts to patronage. I'm grateful to early readers of the manuscript—Charlie Altieri, Tess Gallagher, and Ellen Bryant Voigt—whose discernments helped to shape the book. Without the M.F.A. Program for Writers (now at Warren Wilson College) and its company of passionate intelligences, teaching would have meant isolation from, instead of reinvigorations in, the community of working artists. I am lucky to have known the writers I've met there over the years.

And as I'm alone *en route* so much, I owe my sense of home to Eastport, Maine, its hospitality and singular beauty; and to a few friends with staying power (Gregory Biss, Karen Tepfer, Leslie Bowman, Elliot Fishbein). They feel like family (a comfort whose more conventional forms my life isn't likely ever to afford me). They bear my absences and presences, and keep the faith. It's for them that I want to be good.

Contents

i

Poem

It was from Adam's side
that Eve was drawn.
But when her life is done
where does she go to die?

Will Adam be her tomb?
When she needs that repose rest
will there be any room
in a man so closed?

after Rilke

Women vs men

In a World of Taking, the Mistake

self-esteem
or affection
to take a liking

Down and down into your own regard
you double, dangling a bucket,
to take a shine. What's the secret?
You're not interested in anything

there's only one of. So the mirror
is amazing, and you find yourself inside it
to be deep. If you had another
fifty years, you'd feel no less

this wonderment at being—
framed in a standstill, your head
in the clouds, your likeness in mind—
you could fall in love with reason. This

is the mistake. You think too much
of your life, far from oceans, far
from rivers, far from streaming. You think,
Death I could bear, if it's anything like

this self in the calm of a held pail.
But the catch in the clarity comes then.
To look like this, you mustn't ever
be touched or moved again . . .

beauty v. stasis

self-indulgent

Two Loves

The backhoe braces itself against itself
with two flat feet, and fights
its appetite—I love that
shovel undermining just

[handwritten annotation: backhoe must lean on solid ground but the shovel tills]

the terra firma which its hinder parts
rely on. So the man in me is making
inroads everywhere (great cities rise
where he has wrecked the gardens) while the woman in me

without whom he can't make any headway anyway
has stayed her ground with equal force.
The latitudes of play
are ampler for the rules; the clouds look clearer

in a lake than not; did poets live this long
to practise birth control? Excited by a simile, they take
the indecorum of a stagnant ditch, and make
a mirror of it. Meanwhile it's the backhoe man

who reads. At lunch he hunches over
his *Inquirer*, which is full of
spiritual facts of life, like
MALE GIRL GETS SELF PREGNANT, and he loves it.

Spot in Space and Time

*

Despite his name, the dog's
an imposition—lying in the kitchen, begging in the bedroom,
with his lousy posture and unseemly salivation—
even Pavlov's dog exposes us (as men are known
by companies they keep). At least a dog cannot
expose himself—thank God it takes
some clothing to do that.

*

The chicken in its coop, the chicken in its roasting pan,
the chicken in its place, I mean, with
ruffles of parsley at its ankles, doesn't seem
indecent. Then you sit it up
on the edge of a table and cross
its legs and look: it's naked.

*

The indignant have a word
they cannot say alone: here here.
The soothers say: there there.
The dog's confused. He's neither
fowl nor fish. He cannot go to Esalen
and find himself; he scowls into the new
communications dish.

*

Remember how you dropped
that barbecued rib in your lap,
that casual affair in ninety-eight,

where everyone wore white? Remember how the girls were all
named Faith and Prudence then? Today the supermarket carts
    are full
of little Melodies and Heathers. Virtue's gotten
mild, to say the least. That's pretty
good, the mother says, that's
pretty pretty. Grandma
falls asleep, and there
the doghouse has a child.

        *

Between the looking forward and remembering, it's hard
to find a moment for the present.
I remember space from when
it was a nothing.
Now we understand it's full,
with very little room for vacancy.
The latest limit on the emptiness was on
the radio today: what's not, said scientists,
is smaller than we thought. (Perhaps it is the thought

they're measuring, as everything we know must fit
inside the temples where a sky, by God, is understandable. It
is not isn't nothing faith
we cannot imagine—nothing
is the very stuff of faith. It's *something*
we've forgotten, something
we are missing, in our human
grade and groove. The thinker
stands still, thinking of himself, while there
(in his abandoned microscope)
a million mountains move.

thinking vs. imagination

live in the
present
w/ awareness

Wicked Riff

Sky cloth hung on a church fence, that's
the ticket—bolted in blue, struck with a stick,
it's a mixed lot of luck and a small razzmatazz,
it's a measure of standards, medicinal brandy.
The altar boy's altered, and man, he can jazz.

So the ripple runs right
through the rig's spine and hide.
On a roll with the setters, we love sunny mud.
Generation's spontaneous, given the time;
evolution—can't help it, can't hurt it

and heavy things fly—all those backlogs
of nuns, all those company presidents,
pints of O positive, tonnage of yens—
from the palm comes a Hollywood hell,
from the pyramid somebody's

unclosing eye. Did the world
start to nod? Was I hit where it hurts?
I saw stars unencumbered by
wishes at last—where no story lines mated
the gods and the beasts. You can't sing
in a rut, you can't love
in absentia. Ask me whatever's
the trick to this music, like how
push the buttons and

when take the breath, I'll say lady
you can't take
a course in a feeling.
The horse has to fly.
Don't you beat it to death.

Your Face

Who can pose, or repose,
in the heart's heat? Not the man
at the mike, not the girl at the moment

of utter irrevocability—O
what's a mouth, fallen open
on no part of speech, what's the meaning

of eyes, closed when feeling is deep? Isn't passion
contortion? The love that you want
can't be had in a sense: it's too huge

for a hand, it's too far for a foot. Don't come
measuring moments with me; don't go asking your mirror
how much is this look. Do you take it,

the face, to be yours? At what cost?
Think again, and you're two.
Look again, and you're lost.

thinking v. looking

The Amenities

[handwritten: Pleasantries / Courteous / Desirable]

I owe you an explanation.
My first memory isn't your own
of an empty box. My babyhood cabinets held
a countlessness of cakes, my backyard rotted
into apple glut, windfalls
of money tree, mouthfuls of fib.

At puberty I liked the locks, I made them fast;
the yelling in the hallways was about
lost money or lost love, but not
lost life. Or so
I see it now: in those days
I romanticized a risk (I thought I'd die
in the alcoholic auto, die at the hands
of nerveless dentistry). Small hearts
were printed in the checkbook; when my parents
called me dear, they meant expensive.

Where were you in all that time? Out looking
for your father's body? Making for
your mother's room? I got my A's
in English, civics, sweetness and light; you got
black eyes, and E's, and nowhere fast.
By 1967 when we met (if you could call it
making an acquaintance, rape) I was   *[handwritten: —false favors]*
a maladjusted gush, a sucker for placebos.
Walking home from Central Square, I had
the good girl's petty dread: the woman
to whose yard you dragged me
might detect us, and be furious.

[handwritten: Paradox- amenities]

11

More than anything else, I wanted
no one mad at me. (Propriety, or was it
property, I thought to guard: myself I gave away.)

And as for you, you had the shakes,
were barely seventeen yourself, too raw
to get it up (I said don't be afraid,
afraid of what might happen if you failed).
And afterwards, in one of those moments
it's hard to tell funny from fatal, you did
a terrible civility: you told me

thanks. I'll never forget that moment all my life.
It wasn't until then, as you were
sheathing it to run,
I saw the knife.

Vacation

The sand burns.
The afternoon takes
hours. Men and women
strip to knotted strings

and oil themselves—they come
between her and the sea.
The hundred-thousand-dollar
houses tremble

in the distance,
maybe even
in her mind. But that
is fixable—that's why

she's here: the sky
a stationary blue
for planes to write upon,
the benches bolted

to the walks, the old men
staring steadily, and watches
shining clear as day in towels—
everything is fixable

except the sea, which
touches, and is touched, and breaks.

13

A Cup of Sky, a Foot of Fire

I'm not the one I was,
pedestrian, thirteen, too scared to speak
to the carload of men that slowed down on the country road.
I'm not the one who studied
languages at embassies, but knew
the rudiment was blood. And not the one
who swam straight up into the air
from the happiness of a tramp.
I'm not the one who lived for you, and even now
I'm not the one I was last night, rocking
and rocking myself for fear.

I couldn't kill the starfish,
even to send it to your hand. To its own element,
the dark, it sidelonged back, it sawed slow curves
till it was out of the box of my sight,
and out of light, which is my kind
of grasp, my handsome. What a death

each death is. Day and night someone bewails
some other one, who went away, and stars in droves
come swimming down. A man may pass
before the feeling does. For we were billions
when we loved each other. When we loved each other
we were one. I'm not the one I was.

ii

The Magician

His eye-holes are empty. He utters
a corresponding word and then
dry silence bears the muffled sound
of a fertility, a flood . . .

Does he arouse or arrest it?
Who's in control—the magician?
A fatal fact could be conceived to finish
such a calling-forth, or such a holding-back.

A word's an act, and no one can recover it.
Sometimes the thing we name
suddenly becomes . . . what? a being, almost
human, that the very calling kills.

after Rilke

language

I Knew I'd Sing

A few sashay, a few finagle.
Some make whoopee, some
make good. But most make
diddly-squat. I tell you this

is what I love about
America—the words it puts
in my mouth, the mouth where once
my mother rubbed

a word away with soap. The word
was *cunt*. She stuck that bar
of family-size in there
until there was no hole to speak of, so

she hoped. But still
I'm full of it—the cunt,   *parents*
the prick, short u, short i,
the words that stood

for her and him. I loved   *sex*
the thing they must have done,
the love they must have made, to make
an example of me. After my lunch of Ivory I said

vagina for a day or two, but knew
from that day forth which word struck home
the more like sex itself.
I knew when I was big I'd sing

a song in praise of cunt—I'd want
to keep my word, the one with teeth in it.
Even after I was raised, I swore
nothing but nothing would be beneath me.

list above
say what she wants

Unrepresentative

It's not the artist's place
to capture the world. Where
would you keep it—in a glass of stars,
a bag of stones? Where do you keep
amazement, in a heart? Of course not. Things

death

will be moving, even after
you decide they're dead,
and no carved angel on a rock, no box
importantly belied with fur, can make
the moving stop. I'm warning you, who go around

money

with mirrors, meaning
to catch your breath, you who are used to having
a moon on hand. Between the thumb and forefinger, it turns
to petty change, a quarter, more or less, where poor
imaginations put a man.

Have or Love

As if we had time, and could save it,
sang to keep it,
loved to make it.

As if all the thens on earth were aiming
only for our local now, our own
pet moment (when your head is underwater

any puddle is a flood). The tears don't earn
their name until you shed them—
they're a kind of money, meaningless

till parted with. Could I have ever
been so rich? I gave myself away the day
I gave him up for dead, as if

all possibilities were two—we loved
for good or loved for ill, we worked for life
or stalled for time. As if I made the choice

to sing, or could.

Point of Origin

*

They feed me and feed me and feed me
till the last
passions of the airport parting
are as far away
as Earth. The cruelties, the furies of
recrimination, even love
will pass. In a minute
it's an hour ago.
Varieties of cloud go by,
varieties of blue. There's always
sun somewhere,
a clear to swear by, and I do.

*

Because we argued to the very ramp,
because I was the last to board,
because a man of many years (nobody knew
his language) occupied
my given seat, I get
to go first class. A present!
And the presents multiply, till soon
I am mistaking luck for privilege—I taste
a couple of lunches, have my little weep
in private, take a glass of wine to make
abstractions of, in geometric light.
But all the while behind me there
where calm cannot be bought, where I
was meant to stay,
somebody's baby
cries and cries and cries,
impossible to pacify. . . .

Gray Day

The wheel went round and left me
on a block of broken bottles,
spirits spent. So where

was the Los Angeles we dreamed of, model
for the others, with its ideal
tree (unmitigated lime, pure pear)?

Through swollen eyes I added lots
of blue to everywhere—beyond the tattoo parlor
bloomed a slough of lower hopes—I got myself

a permanent, I paid a dude to shoot
two pearls into my ears (somewhere
an oyster's sore) but still

the trees were shade trees—eyeshade, dayshade,
green made gray by evening, and not
an orange or a plum in sight, no apple

for an eye. It's midnight now, and maybe you
could send me just a shiver or an inkling
of a message, huh? I used to think

the colors added up
to black—that's how alike
some opposites can be. You came

as easy as you went. The virgin's
deep in tears. The widow's
innocent.

What Could Hold Us

Hats divide generally into three classes: offensive hats,
defensive hats, and shrapnel.
　　　　　　　—KATHERINE WHITEHORN

i

There are no accidents, or so
the lucky like to say.
In the department store she ran
smack into the clutches of
an unassuming man, and double-breasted them.
She drew away at once, but saw
he looked aghast at being
implicated so—with his offending
hands in air—they never meant
to take such liberties—and all around
stood mannequins, unmoved,
in shades of innocence,
in underwear.

ii

In the togetherness department, stores
leave much to be desired. The couches seem malposed
beside the barbecues, the bicycles beside the bras,
the customers beside
themselves, or reasonable
facsimiles.

iii

She hauled the bedroom suite to the public dump
where one man's paid to stay all day and oversee
the afterlife of wealth. She saw what trucks and trunks
delivered: headless dolls, dead televisions, tangles
of forgetful lamp, a signmaker's
unwanted ampersands. And over everything
the dump man passed, with mercy
and a yellow *machina* (it's he
who parts the earth, who heals the wound,
who tends the jilted and who calms the dead). She stood there
by the empty pickup while he dozed
the king-size thing and earth together,
burning and the bed.

iv

However big the pain, the earth can take it.
Habeas corpus, the raincoat wraps
the flasher's trouble up. Habits close about the nun's
uncustomary hurt. The earth's big headache (having so many
of us in mind) is soothed
by a pacifist sky, with a bright blue sash or a few white flags
or a green forgiving rain, whatever suits the hidden
haberdasher . . .

Professional Hazard

The best in human beauty's not
so distant from the ordinary—yet
we spend our lives on such
small differences.

On money, to buy envy,
futures, to buy time. At times the very words
in my mouth belittle me, but still
there's something big, I swear—

or do I plead? (No fundamentalism understands
this kinship, between blasphemy and prayer—
in either, and in both, we know
the ultimate's about
the middle.) As

for everlasting, love to have it
your way, have to love it. Either way
it's going fast. We don't
know much, and are
professors of it.

Capital

For a second the word express appears
in apposition to the word espresso (that's
what happy is about) and then

the bus is gone from the coffee-house door.
Again you're in the luckless world, world
without fortune, where you swear to do
something unspeakable
if one more person mentions consciousness.
Along the street lie bikes and beggars,
honestly broke or crookedly OK;
at corners, stalled around a smoke
the children of boards and clubs look about
as expressive as wood. So what
do a hundred thousand people need

each other for? A public to be private in?
The fifth amendment, which you have to have
a hearing to invoke? A party for a landslide,
circulation for the Times? Don't ask,

says the cop on the beat. Keep your mind
on the change, says the street musician. Sure enough,
his dark blue velvet box, impressed
with the withdrawn
clarinet, attracts
a small downfall of dimes.

Bear in English

The animal is the act, the keeper says.
He's read his Yeats. He has
a Ph.D. in Zen. He's fixed
the communist flamingos with
his pinking shears, and given all
the monkeys mirrors and allowances.
I'm told to play the sax like mad—a crowd
adores the blues.
                           But where
are others like myself, who feel
the heaviness of human names—the weight
of withers, muzzle, rib cage, balls? Are bodies only
what the keeper says—a little occupation
for the mind? At night the brilliant parallelograms

slide through my sleeping-room, unhampered
by the humped domestications I was once
so taken with. On Sundays, consolation gets
dished out (like "Nothing actually exists").
A slave is given everything
a slave could need—his gravy and his glasses,
lumps to love and roofs to look up to.
The keeper says this is
the life—it never snows, it never rains—
but Christ, without a sky, I can't

have faith. I studied every day for years
between the acts, to learn
his words for free, for once
and for all. But in his sentences were only two
varieties of voice, their premises the same.

They need each other,
overlord and underdog,
and I became him,
as the mink became his wife. I mean

language has turned
into my only way to know.
I've found the words
and what they say

is "Do not let me go."

Constructive

You take a rock, your hand is hard.
You raise your eyes, and there's a pair
of small beloveds, caught in pails.
The monocle and eyepatch correspond.

You take a glove, your hand is soft.
The ocean floor was done
in lizardskin; around a log or snag
the surface currents run

like lumber about a knot. A boat
is bent to sea—we favor the medium
we're in, our shape's
around us. It takes time. At night,

the bed alive, what
teller of truth could tell
the two apart? Lover, beloved,
hope is command. Your hand

is given, when you take a hand.

Relative

theory of matter + motion

In and out of the light of trees
move people, jacketed bright and brown;

behind them moves the mountain, in and out
of clouds; above it all the sun is supposed

to be up and around. It all depends
on something unconfessed, of course,

myself, of course, considering myself
at rest. I mean what's up? What's in? The answer is _of our_

perceptions of our mind.

the answerer, a fashion, a position,
and the whole night long on the highway, moved, I'll have

a moon to keep me company, as still
as I am, in the glass, while trees and signs and homes
   keep racing

toward the past. What's staying
anyway? What's going on? It is

ourselves, ourselves. Turning my back,
I said that _you_ had gone.

Imagery

_We take abstract matter to
categorizes it - couplets 4 -5._

_I said you left, but
really I pulled away from you._ 31

What Poems Are For

They aren't for everything.
I better swallow this, or else
wind up shut up by openness so utter.
Nip and tuck, poems are for

a bit, a patch, a mended hem, carnation's cage—and then
the heart may bloom, the sex may roar,
the moment widen to be the well
the child fell in forever, yes—but not until

I've checked the pinafore and laced the meat,
puttied the stones and pinched the flowers back.
I can't give you a word to hold the dead. I can't give you
the name of God, a big enough

denomination. Find yourself
a church instead, where roofs are all allusions
to the sky, and words are all
incorrigible. I can't give you

timelessness, or time. I have
a spoon, a bed, a pen, a hat. The poem
is for something, and the world
is small. I'll give you that.

iii

Sacred Law

How powerfully the Pope, in the depths of his fast
(without being any less venerable,
according to the sacred law of contrast)
has to attract the devil.

Maybe we reckon too little
with the shifting balance:
there are currents in the Tiber River,
every move incurs a counter-move.

I remember Rodin
telling me one day with a cocky air
(we were at Chartres, taking the train)
that being too pure, the cathedral provoked

winds of disdain.

after Rilke

Animal Song

The fox knows many things, but the hedgehog knows one big thing.
—ARCHILOCHUS

We're flattered they come so close,
amused when they resemble us,
amazed when they do not.
The animal we named the sex fiend for
has no known family but ours. The angels,
on the other hand, can be identified
by something birds in any small backyard are largely
made of. If we do not move
perhaps they will approach us, in the spirit

of unearthing something. Everywhere inside the ground
are avenues and townships of
another world, enormously minute. And when we harbor
some largesse—the feeling of a blue sky no one knows
where starts or stops—then for a moment
we don't terrify the animals. It's rare, but it
can happen. Someday, when the something

greater than our lives has come, perhaps we'll stop our digging
little definitions for a hole. Perhaps we shall recall
the language in which we were intimate—before we called

the creature names. We'd have to talk with it, remembering
the way
animal comes from soul, and not
its opposite.

Take Care

When a man dies, he does not die just
of the disease he has; he dies of his whole life.
                                    —CHARLES PÉGUY

Our neighbor Laura Foley used to love
to tell us, every spring when we returned
from work in richer provinces, the season's
roster of disease, bereavement, loss. And all
her stars were ill, and all her ailments worth
detailing. We were young, and getting up
into the world; we feigned a gracious
interest when she spoke, but did
a slew of wicked imitations, out
of earshot. Finally her bitterness drove off
even such listeners as we, and one by one the winters nailed
more cold into her house, until the decade crippled her,
and she was dead. Her presence had been
tiresome, cheerless, negative, and there was little
range or generosity in anything she said. But now that I   *to list*

have lost my certainty, and spent my spirit in a waste
of one romance, I think enumerations have their place,
descriptive of what keeps on keeping on. For dying's nothing
simple, single; and the records of the odd demises
(stone inside an organ, obstacles to brook,
a pump that stops, some cells that won't, the fevers making
mockeries of lust) are signatures of lively
interest: they presuppose
a life to lose. And if the love of life's   *seriousness*
an art, and art is difficult, then we   *= real love*
were less than laymen at it (easy come
is all the layman knows). I mean that maybe
Laura Foley loved life more, who kept
so keen an eye on how it goes . . .

The Trouble with "In"

In English, we're in trouble.
Love's a place
we fall into, so
sooner or later they ask

How deep? Time's a measure
of extent, so sooner or later they ask
How long? We keep
some comforters inside a box,
the heart inside a chest, but still

it's there the trouble with the dark
accumulates the most. The end of life
is said to be
a boat to a tropic, good

or bad. The suitor wants
to size up what
he's getting into, so
he gets her measurements. But how much

is enough? The best man cannot
help him out—he's given to his own
uncomfortable cummerbund.
Inside the mirror, several bridesmaids
look and look, in the worst half-light,

too long, too little, not enough alike,
and who can stand to be
made up for good? And who can face
being adored? I swear

there is no frame
that I would keep you in.
I didn't love a shape
and later find you fit it—
every day your sight was a surprise;
you made my taste, made sense,
made eyes. But when you set me up

in high esteem, I was a star
that's bound, in time,
to fall. The bound's
the sorrow of the song. I loved you

to no end, and when you said
So far, I knew the idiom:
it meant So long.

What We Call Living

i

His watch is wicked, going on
without him. Pass your hand
across the blue man's lips and
Q.E.D. We know we breathe

and quite without our help, but then
we know we know, and so forget.
It's strange to be alive but we
have not felt awe since we were someone's

kid, and that was once
upon a time. In time we taught ourselves
to find the world mundane, and all
the unknown unsurprising, like

next Sunday, for example. God himself
gets bored, God knows.

ii

On holidays we like to make
some sugar on a rope, some fallout
in the form of rocks, a Science City someone gave
to Junior, Christmas Day. And we can etch
our name in the petri dish with pure
bacteria, or in the virgin snow with piss.
We put our signature on everything—we draw the line
at skin for different, at heart for dead; but now and then

the EKG machine goes on
all by itself. There was a time
we really sang, forgetting differences, and when we did
the air itself would seem alive—but then

we fell back into dream; our definitions froze.
Tonight all night the household's bolted dead,
the family's fast asleep. But in the drawing room
the crystal grows.

To God or Man

A line's not meant to lie there, longing
to be thralled into a coil. Give me a spike

in my EKG. The moment's meant
to jump, the moon return, the drumhouse

roll us all around. Send down
a lassoist or flute. And though

it means some truck with death
(to whom I know

the spoils belong) I need
a shipment of your special fruit,

a flatbed of your basic seed.
In this, the country of

the angel and the witch (the underworld
a shadow of above), I see

at most and least a wing, I miss
the long and short of love. I've sent

this message out as many nights
as Zeno said it takes

to add the half-lives up.
The river holds the sky and yet

it moves;
where does the blue begin?

(You needn't answer
in a word or flash—

the water stays and still
the wave comes in . . .)

Down, Down and Down

After seven months in space, the astronauts
sank back into the blues that blanket earth.
We saw them land, we saw them trundled
from their second home, and then

we saw they couldn't stand—they couldn't
hold a bunch of flowers up, the world
had got so heavy. So the story they had starred in
turned from legendary tale (The Music of the Spheres)

to sorry verité (The Newsreels of Their New Wheelchairs).
So much for weightlessness as grace;
for months thereafter, none of them
could sleep: they told us down was hard.

        *

My first twelve thousand nights on earth
went fast. I always had
a quilt or a religion or a man,
some comforters of dream, the stars sewn up

along a storyteller's lines. My life
was always looking up, I always had
a little always in my bag. So what
befell? Did I get old? Does everyone warm-blooded start

to feel this cold? Sometimes I think I'll think
the vacancy away—I tell myself there is a trick, time's
weather, for example, in Marseilles. By then I've passed
no more than thirty of

the eighty-seven thousand seconds in a day.
It doesn't help to know
a number—time on earth's
no code, it won't be cracked. The man I loved

is just as lost as ever, and for that
no hill or hole, no president or anchorman
has pull enough. My bluest moons and oceans don't
mean anything to him. He won't come back.

Or Else

In memoriam: Mitchell Toney *[died of AIDS]*

What could we say to you
while you died? Could we
say stay? Who, after all,
was moving? All my life

I dealt in words, but now
I should listen, just shut up and listen,
by the ditch of silver, by the uninvested moon—
all night among *[coffin in grave.]*

the wealth of speechless elements,
where unlit earth is dumbest.
Listen for the shiver of a sign. Or else
you die both to and from us.

[turns on mirror on herself. the words fail—she must listen]

[light over a patient's bed.]

[She looks for a sign of death, but sees all the things that made him alive — the death itself is an act that made her persevere.]

[She always leaves a paradox at end]

46 *[death]*

The Ghost

I held my breath for years, for fear
of being breathless, fear of being
afraid. Whenever someone left my bed
I took a deeper one. Addicted

to the flesh, attracted to
the very quick, I thought
I'd never let them go (my child,
my man, my love

of home). But lately, in the winter
stoneyards, when the still heaps
hold their blue, and a hand is all
wool thumbs, and no one says

hello, or hello's other half,
and stars, above all, after all,
strike fire from the lapidary slope—
then something rises

out of me at last—my hope
and heat, the spirit I
had trusted most. We have to give up
everything of love—even the ghost.

All About Us

The animal is ravenously
nimbostratus—all about and eating up
the blue, and all the while
inside. It has the power to burn
the world in a flash, to blacken
four skies in a wink, to sound
with a stick, to lick with a look, to feel
with all our might. My mind, which made

so much of a man, is changed. I see the light
not in but as your eyes, I take my sense
of fine construction from your hand,
and move from wanting's house. And as I wander

this holds fast: you are my true and my magnetic,
animal, my astral map. The whirl of garment
all about the earth is breath—in oceans made
of air, the shell's a telephone, the coil's
a curiosity, the cell a billion years across.
An animal's an outburst, with a steeple in
the structure of the hands. I'm looking up the heavens

never resident in words.
I wonder, Spirit, will you quell
or animate the torch's thirst?

iv

Two Poems after Rilke

(To a Woman)

My friend, I must leave you.
Do you want to see
the place on a map?
It's a black dot.

Inside myself, if things
all go as planned,
it will become a point of rose
in a green land.

(The fruit is heavier to bear)

The fruit is heavier to bear
than flowers seem to be.
But that's a lover talking,
not a tree.

To the Quick

We fixed the ages of the irises at flower,
stopped the eons of the oranges at fruit.
Ripe was ready, since we liked to eat,
and beautiful was full by virtue of
the ear-eye-nose-and-throat man.
Time was sometimes said
to be at hand.

But not for a second
did the plant stand still.
The space we designated blooming—when
did it begin? The beans turned white
to green, and green to brown, and then
were no less Phaseolus; flesh
fell off into enormous
gravity, and seeds
were an end in themselves, in a way. On top

of the TV set I put
the baby pictures, meant to keep
the little person as he was, as still
as he could be. O man, o child,
we loved each other less

for how we moved
than how we stayed. But what
did we adore about the river?
Its unfixed address and vagaries of bed.

Bar and Grill

The world the window held
was stirred—itself
was liquid, thickened slightly
toward the ground, where fast

pedestrians were passing by
and busses struck from silver mints
and bicycles well-spoken, and the host
of esses, nesses, motion making

individuals abstract, as motion will;
and then the window bound them
to the ground a bit, it
warped and rippled them, it drew them out—

however reticent the tucked dress was, it had
to bleed a little down; however pinned to stripe the suit
it spilled an eyelet in the eyecup of
the bar and grill I saw them from; is this

unclear? I was attracted
to the glasses there, some full
of purple corked, some pure
unstoppered mud, and all about

what disappears. Whoever leaves revises
everybody else's eyes.
You will not see me any more, that's why
the world cannot stop moving.

A Physics

When you get down to it, Earth
has our own great ranges
of feeling—Rocky, Smoky, Blue—
and a heart that can melt stones.

The still pools fill with sky,
as if aloof, and we have eyes
for all of this and more, for Earth's
reminding moon. We too are ruled

by such attractions—spun and swaddled,
rocked and lent a light. We run
our clocks on wheels, our trains
on time. But all the while we want

to love each other endlessly—not only for
a hundred years, not only six feet up and down.
We want the suns and moons of silver
in ourselves, not only counted coins in a cup. The whole idea

of love was not to fall. And neither was
the whole idea of God. We put him well
above ourselves, because we meant,
in time, to measure up.

When Does It Happen?

For the child in Marshall MacLuhan's account,
who, on his first plane ride, sat silent as the plane took off,
and silent as it reached its cruising altitude and silent
several minutes more, before turning to his father to ask,
"When do we start getting smaller?"

        *

When the dog and hunter float
in a corrective curve,
and never meet the bear.

When the man-made pool
begins to whirl, in forever's
wink of an eye.

The phosphorescences are drunk, the starfish
love us, lap us up. When do we start
to get small? When the baby is big.

        *

The longer we want, the littler the wishes become.
Their numbers grow, we have
to have, till even love

is understood as made. (Your favorite
cake, concocted on a mountaintop,
has failed to rise. You weigh

the rulebook, asking, Is it done? What
etiquette!) The children look
like their mother. See how they close their eyes?

*

A watch sails into space,
a yardstick going fast enough
is only one foot long, so put

your best foot forward, spin the whole
rotunda, make the planets play. There's something
before the child, and something after the adult—

do we live twice? is midnight opposite of noon?
when do I get my present? (Never
is the answer now; always is the answer soon.)

Big Ideas Among Earthlings

Who'd want to be the biggest one,
the president or mastermind,
the lord of stars or model of
the kind? Who'd want the drove

of sycophants, the plague
of elitists and angels, echoing
her every word? A little
loam and nightsoil

is a lot—the miles unfurl inside
a single iris, small hours
in hot purple, wet gotten
from eavesdropping.

    *

We craved our own lost halves
ever since language and land
were sundered into kind.
And Africa misses

South America, and clouds
their coast. And to this day I love
the fucker who deserted me, but who
can claim to hold a soul—even her own? Americans think big

is forceful, but the strongest force belongs
to the electrons (bound, at 40,000 mph, about
their far-off nuclei); from them we get our sense
that matter's solid. You can look

about, above, for lords and kings. But given
what we know of strangeness, given what we know of charm,
perhaps the god is small, not big,
who keeps us from harm.

The Matter Over

It is better to say "I am suffering" than
to say "This landscape is ugly."
SIMONE WEIL

From the piling's kelp I drew
the starfish with its five blunt fingers.

First I thought the creature
less than handsome, less of a hand

than I expected, rigid, with a stumpy gray
asymmetry of grasp. It wasn't soft. It hardly moved. So maybe

it was dead? I couldn't see
beyond myself, until I turned

the matter over, and beheld
billions of unfamiliar

facts—minute transparent
footlets, feelers, stems

all waving to the quick, and then
the five large radials beginning

gradually to flail, in my slow sight,
and then, in my thin air,

to drown. I'd meant
to send it, as a gift, to you

who were my missing part,
so far inland. Instead

59

to a world the sighted have no rights to,
to the dark that's out of mind,

I made myself resign it,
flinging the hand from my hand.

About the Author

Heather McHugh works in cities half the year, doing public readings and residencies, and spends the rest of her time at home in the island community of Eastport, Maine. Before *To the Quick*, she published two other books of poetry, *Dangers* and *A World of Difference*, and one translation, *D'Après Tout: Poems by Jean Follain*. McHugh is a graduate of Radcliffe College (B.A. 1969) and of the University of Denver (M.A. 1972). She has received two NEA fellowships. Since 1975 she has taught in the non-residential M.F.A. Program for Writers, now affiliated with Warren Wilson College. In 1985 she was appointed Milliman Writer-in-Residence at the University of Washington in Seattle, and in 1987 the Holloway Lecturer in Poetry at the University of California at Berkeley.